*Life L*
*from*

# MELROSE PL.

## ANTHONY RUBINO, JR.

Adams Media Corporation
HOLBROOK, MASSACHUSETTS

Published by Adams Media Corporation
260 Center Street, Holbrook, MA 02343

ISBN: 1-55850-598-9
Printed in Canada.
First Edition
J I H G F E D C B A

Rubino, Anthony, 1966-
Life lessons from Melrose Pl. / Anthony Rubino, Jr.
p.   cm.
ISBN 1-55850-598-9 (pbk.)
1. Melrose Place (Television program)   I. Title
PN1992.77.M44R8   1996
791.45'72—dc20

95-51219
CIP

*This book is available at quantity discounts for bulk purchases. For information, call 1-800-872-5627.*
*Visit our home page at http://www.adamsmedia.com*

*T*o my current wife, Colleen—who dragged me, kicking and screaming, to the couch each week and forced me to watch *Melrose Place*.
Now . . . if only she had a sister . . .

*S*peaking of sisters . . .
also, to Cara and Maria

## ACKNOWLEDGMENTS

Very special thanks to Darren Star,
*Melrose Place* creator, and Aaron Spelling,
MP producer.

Thanks to my special MP consultants
Bethany Stancliff and Beth Weinberg.

# CONFESSIONS OF A PLACE-AHOLIC

Hello . . . My name is Tony . . . and I watch *Melrose Place*.

It wasn't always this way. I used to spend my time doing other things on Wednesday nights, and now, Mondays— I used to read, work, even watch other TV shows. But not anymore.

I blame my wife . . . she drove me to it . . . she's always been a TV enabler. Hell, even before we were married she tried to get me hooked on *Knots Landing*. But I was able to keep that under control. Oh sure . . . I was a casual viewer. I'd watch an episode now and then to relax, but that was all it ever amounted to. But *Melrose* . . . *Melrose was different*.

It all started during the second season. Like a lot of *Place*-aholics, the first season didn't have much of an effect on me. It was somehow easier to resist—less potent. During that second season, though, my wife would tune in religiously each week. Soon thereafter, her diabolic, weekly seduction would begin.

"Come on," she'd say. "Just watch a little bit. I'm watching . . . all our friends are watching . . . everybody's doing it . . . You're not cool if you don't watch." I'd try to resist by telling her I was concerned it would lead to other shows. "Oh, come on!" she'd say. "It's not like occasionally watching *Melrose* is going to get you hooked on *daytime* soaps, or anything! It's just *Melrose Place*. . . . It's not *All My Children,* for God's sake!"

Eventually, her persistent luring proved impossible to resist. At first I'd make excuses. "I'm only watching this because Heather Locklear is in a bikini," I'd say. Or sometimes I wouldn't allow myself to sit down while viewing the program—as if I were only passing by, and happened to glance at the TV. Then, when a commercial would air, I'd exclaim, "OH, HOW CAN YOU WATCH THIS CRAP?!" and storm from the room . . . only to return and repeat my charade until the next commercial break. Who was I kidding? I was already hooked, and I knew it.

Finally I gave up all attempts at resistance and began to watch on a regular basis. Not only was I sitting through entire episodes, but I found myself intrigued by the characters' undaunted resilience, and fascinated by the sheer volume of adversity overcome each hour. *Explosions . . . murder . . . seductions . . . blackmail . . . deceit . . . molestation . . . occasional bad hair . . . water retention!* To the residents of *Melrose Place,* that's a slow day . . . Hell, that's a *slow morning!* They deal with seemingly insurmountable and devastating life crises more quickly and casually than most of us can put on socks.

So I began to think, wouldn't it be great if we could use some of the life lessons they implement every day—crushing menacing adversaries and advancing their careers with head-spinning velocity—and apply them the next time we try to talk our way out of a speeding ticket or explain why we're late for work? Wouldn't you love to be armed with Amanda's confidence and fortitude, or Jake's "rebel-without-a-cause" assertiveness, the next time you have to deal with a minor life crisis? The way I see it, we stand to learn a lot from a group of people who navigate, largely unscathed, through dozens of overwhelming obstacles on an hourly basis—all the while looking really good and having tremendous amounts of sex.

It was with this in mind that I decided to write the definitive book of *Melrose Place* philosophy—an examination of the messages, advice, and life lessons found in each and every episode of one of the most popular television programs of our time.

As you ponder the slightly unorthodox, yet strangely practical Melrosian wisdom that graces the following pages, I encourage you to find deeper meaning hidden in each entry. And I invite you to confer with your friends, and other fans, in trying to recall which episode inspired each pearl.

So, for now, my fellow *Place*-aholics: If you're a woman, take the hem up two inches on the shortest skirt you own . . . if you're a guy, put on some tight pants and *take your shirt off, for heaven's sake* . . . now, pour yourself some fine, chilled champagne, domestic beer, or a 22-ounce glass of straight vodka, sit back in your modest yet amazingly trendy apartment, turn the page, and escape, for a little while, to 4616 Melrose Place. After all, you deserve a little diversion, because sometimes life can be a *really big bitch*. But that's OK. Because with the help of this book . . . so can you.

# THE MPMCWUQ
## (MELROSE PLACE MULTIPLE CHOICE WARM-UP QUIZ)

To help you fully appreciate the valuable wisdom and life lessons in this book, you must first establish a link between your world and the world of *Melrose Place*. You have to be able to picture yourself responding to ordinary situations as if you were a member of the MP cast. To help you achieve this, here is a multiple-choice warm-up exercise.

Read the following scenario depicting a somewhat common, minor life crisis, followed by several hypothetical reactions. Each of these reactions corresponds to the way a character on *Melrose Place* might respond in a similar "real life" situation. See if you can identify which character is most likely to have each reaction.

**Good luck!**

You are in your car, stopped at a red light, when suddenly a man in a black Mercedes rear-ends you. You and the man driving the Mercedes exit your vehicles and check the point of impact, finding some minor damage to your bumper, but no damage to his. You then suggest that you both exchange license and registration information. The man sneers at you and proceeds to get back in his car, intending to drive away.

**What would you do?**

### Response #1
Retrieve a blunt object from the back seat of your car and bludgeon the man within an inch of his life.

### Response #2
Stop the man, and seductively invite him back to your apartment. Once there, sleep with him, while photographing the encounter. The next day, mail copies of the photos to the man's office. Tell him that you'll send those same pictures to his wife if he does not agree to replace your bumper *and* have your car cleaned at a reputable, brushless car wash. Once your car has been cleaned to your satisfaction, make the man buy you a coupon book good for more washes, several hot-wax procedures, and maybe a few undercarriage rust protection treatments (even though you know this is just a useless gimmick dreamed up by greedy car wash proprietors). Then, file the photos away for any future car maintenance needs.

### Response #3
Exhale huskily and say, "Hey . . . Why don't you go where you're watchin'. Hey . . . I'm talking to you . . ." Then watch the guy drive away. Get in your car and drive home, swerving wildly and running over three garbage cans and a cat. When you get home, make yourself a couple more vodka martinis, and pass out.

### Response #4

Say, "Hey pal, You're lucky I was driving my friend's car! If I was on my bike I could've been seriously hurt, man." When he ignores you, grab him by the shoulder, spin him around and clock him with your right hand. When he falls to the ground, shake your hand like you can't believe how hard you just hit the guy, *man*. Then point at him on the ground as he wipes a small droplet of blood from the corner of his mouth with the side of his hand, and say, "You know, it's rich jerks like you that go around thinking it's OK to do anything and say anything you want, drive around in your fancy cars and run down working stiffs like me. Now go on and get outta here before I really get mad and decide not to fix this damaged bumper myself, using my large tool set and extensive knowledge of automotive repair."

### Response #5

Place your hands on your hips and stare at the guy with the only facial expression you seem to be capable of. You know . . . that all-purpose, pouty blank gaze you use to express happiness, anger, fear, loathing, disgust, angst, apathy, lust, desire, surprise, suspicion, contentment, rapture, and fatigue.

### Response #6

Turned on by the man's rebellious bad-boy tendencies, you decide to have his baby. Despite his willingness to help with the infant's upbringing, you insist upon raising the child on your own (damn your strong-willed, independent, woman-of-the-'90s self-reliance!)—only to end up having to shoot the man when you discover the money he used to repair your bumper was from drug trafficking.

### Response #7
Become strangely attracted to the guy for the very fact that he seems to be taking advantage of you. Begin a serious relationship with him, and after about a week, sign documents giving him control of half your business. Then, at his request, buy him a one-way ticket to Venezuela, and transfer all your money into his account so he can "invest it for you." After that, agree to meet him for dinner, and fully expect him to show up.

### Response #8
Just let him go. You're just too damned busy sleeping around, smugly manipulating people, and just being a general rat-bastard to deal with it.

### Response #9
Say, "Aw, it's OK. No harm done, really. Have a nice day!" Then go home, fix somebody's backed-up toilet, make love to your wife, and turn in early.

### Response #10

Ask the guy, nicely, to at least share the cost of the repairs with you. When he is touched by your gesture to share the cost of fixing damages that were clearly his fault, he warms up to you. You end up identifying each other's needs and sensibilities over a cup of coffee, and find that you share many liberal concerns about current social issues. Eventually, you start to date, and for a while it looks as if you are finally going to find happiness as a gay man. But just when you think the general public might be ready to view a homosexual relationship on prime-time television for more than three or four episodes, something goes wrong and you never see the guy again.

### Response #11

Shocked by the man's disrespectful response, despite the fact that you're fully dressed in your regulation police patrolwoman's uniform, you draw your service revolver and tell the man to "freeze" or you'll shoot.

### Response #12

Very calmly, tell the man that if he gets in his car and drives away he will soon regret the day his mother brought him into this world. When he ignores you, simply take down his license plate number, get back into your vehicle, and calmly drive away. That very afternoon, run a check on the license plate on your computer and find out who the man is, where he lives, and which company he owns. Start a rumor that his company is about to file Chapter 11. When the stock price falls, buy up enough shares to be the controlling stockholder, while simultaneously mailing photographs of the guy in bed with another woman to his wife—who subsequently leaves him and takes everything he owns. Then, call a stock-holders' meeting, where the man (a mere shell of what he used to be) will learn for the first time that you are the company's new CEO, when you spin around in your high-backed leather chair and announce that you will be liquidating the company and diverting its assets to a Japanese corporation, one that just happens to manufacture the rear bumper on your car. As the man dissolves into tears, smile and say, "I'd love to stay and chat, but I have to take my car in for repair. Good day, gentlemen." and walk out.

# Answers

Response #1:   Kimberly Shaw

Response #2:   Sydney Andrews

Response #3:   Alison Parker

Response #4:   Jake Hanson

Response #5:   Billy Campbell

Response #6:   Jo Reynolds

Response #7:   Jane Mancini

Response #8:   Michael Mancini

Response #9:   The nice hard-working doctor/superintendent, Michael Mancini, from the first season

Response #10:   Matt Fielding

Response #11:   OOPS! Sorry! That's Officer Stacy Sheridan's response (Heather Locklear's character on T.J. Hooker)

Response #12:   Amanda Woodward (in a good mood)

*DID YOU EVER HAVE ONE OF THOSE DAYS*—when you're wrongly imprisoned for murdering your love interest's wife, right after a co-worker blackmails you into promoting her by threatening to expose the fact that you were previously married and faked your own death . . . and it's all you can do to keep the crease in your freshly pressed, $3000 designer suit and your highly fashionable hairstyle looking pristine, when a leggy, psychotic doctor (with a gruesome head wound) blows up your apartment building . . . and all this is really inconvenient because you were planning to go out that day and spend some of the money you've suddenly come into through a mysterious trust fund, lucrative investment, or highly profitable divorce settlement?

Yeah . . . me neither. But who knows what tomorrow will bring. That's why I've composed the following *Life Lessons from Melrose Place*.

*D*o unto others as you feel like it.

*I*f you love something, set it free.
If it comes back, it's yours. If it doesn't
come back, blackmail it until it does.

*N*o matter what is happening in your life, or in the world around you, always be ready, willing, and able to have mad, passionate sex.

*K*eep gruesome head wounds well covered by a securely fastened, quality wig.

*I*f you wind up in prison, accused of murdering your homosexual lover's wife, don't be too surprised if your parents have difficulty accepting the situation.

*T*ake it one sister at a time.

*D*on't suppress your anger.
Use it to be an even bigger bitch.

*I*f more than, oh . . . say . . . three of your
lovers swindle you out of hundreds
of thousands of dollars, it's time to
reevaluate the people you date.

*M*arry often and swiftly.

*I*f a person rejects you more than three times in a row, it's time to cut your losses and get on with your life.
So have the person killed, and move on.

**W**hen stalking someone, wear comfortable shoes, and remain at least fifty feet behind your victim.

**H**ave sex first, ask questions later.

*I*f you find it difficult to get along with your boss, try to reason with him and talk through your differences. If that doesn't work, drive him to suicide and take over the company.

*W*hen arranging a seedy, covert meeting by telephone, always say, "Come alone, or the deal's off!" right before you hang up.

*I*f you fall off a four-story building, take your brother along with you to break your fall.

$I$f your "significant other" leaves town for more than a week, sleep with whomever you want. After all, you can't be expected to wait around forever.

$W$hen your mother-in-law says your wife is dead, don't take her word for it.

*B*e nice to people until you get what you want from them. Then discard them like pocket lint.

*B*e sure to have a surgeon supervise your psychiatric care.

Give people second and third chances. A person who is ruthless and cruel to you one week might have a complete and total personality change the following week, and be lovable and needy.

*P*ick one person and mess with their head until it no longer amuses you.

*S*ay, "Look . . . ," before every other sentence.

*B*eing a loving husband, hard-working doctor/superintendent, and generally nice guy can turn you into a real rat-bastard in a very short period of time.

*A*lways wear plenty of makeup and hair spray to bed.

*D*on't overreact. For example, if someone inadvertently embarrasses you in public, don't let anger get the best of you. It really isn't necessary to frame the person for a murder he/she didn't commit. Wouldn't it be enough to simply break up his or her marriage instead?

*N*ever sleep with your boss or a co-worker. Just kidding. You should do both, often.

*S*quash the helpless, weak, and vulnerable like bugs.

*I*f you've been married to a woman less than a week, and you catch her in more than ten huge lies, that's a pretty good indication that you've made a mistake.

 *I*f you lose your job, wait a few minutes, and you'll get an even better job at twice the salary.

*H*ooking is an excellent way to earn some spare cash!

*I*f you can't get work hooking, you can also make a nice living stripping.

*I*f you're having marital problems, try communicating more effectively with your spouse. You may even want to consider seeing a marriage counselor. If you don't see results after about three months, have your spouse killed and go to Rio with the insurance money.

*I*t's difficult to deny blowing up a building when, like, ten people saw you do it.

*A* good way to aggravate your sister is to tell her that Mom liked you best. Another good way is to sleep with her husband a bunch of times.

*I*f your wife tries to kill you more than twice, it may be a sign that there are some minor problems with your relationship.

*T*he only thing worse than having the same colossal, super-bitch for a boss and landlord is finding out that she's also sleeping with your boyfriend.

*I*t is never, ever inappropriate to wear an exceedingly revealing outfit with a really short skirt.

*I*f someone annoys you, pick a sensitive issue in their life and use it to snipe something mean and hurtful at them. Who knows . . . you might even make the person cry!

*I*f you help break up your sister's marriage, then trick her ex-husband into marrying you, it's considered bad form to wear her wedding dress to the ceremony.

*S*pend all holidays with your neighbors—never with your family.

*A* good way to unwind after a hard day at the office is to build a fire, curl up with a good book, and rapidly drink seven large glasses of straight vodka.

*B*efore bursting into a crowded holiday party to yell, "CALL 911!" check to make sure you're not naked.

*D*on't judge a good-looking environmentalist from Seattle by his cover.

*I*t's perfectly natural to have cold feet just before your wedding ceremony. But, if these feelings persist, take off your wedding dress, jump out of the window, and bolt.

*I*f you walk into your office first thing in the morning and find your dead boss hanging by the neck above your desk with a note pinned to his shirt, you just know it's gonna be "one of those days."

*D*on't be too quick to fire a disobedient employee. Sometimes it's better to let the person keep their job, and just make their life a living hell.

*P*urses and blowtorches don't mix.

*T*wo wrongs don't make a right—but they're usually good for a few laughs.

*W*ait to see how much money is in the trust fund before you quit your job.

$I$n order to have a successful marriage, you have to communicate with your spouse. However, don't bore your partner with insignificant details, like the fact that you're about to inherit hundreds of thousands of dollars.

*B*eing a regular member of a community for a prolonged period of time may help keep you from harm in the event of a deadly explosion. If you've only been around for a few weeks, your chances of being killed increase significantly.

*J*ust because a person blows up your apartment building and kills someone doesn't mean he or she is a bad person— just a little high-strung.

*I*t's more poignant to share a last quality moment with your dying father than to go get the doctor to save his life.

$I$f you find yourself financially ruined, don't worry. In a few minutes you'll be given a large sum of money, your own business, or a high-paying job. In fact, becoming financially ruined is an excellent way to improve your situation.

*T*o avoid confusing your husband's money (or lack thereof) with your own, keep a secret checking account in a different bank.

*M*artinis!
They're not just for breakfast anymore!

*I*f a friend comes home from rehab, toast her with tasty nonalcoholic beverages. But as soon as she leaves, break out the brewskies and have some real fun.

*A*void relationships with alcoholic, sex-crazed, professional football stars.

*U*se only one tranquilizer capsule to drug your sister. Two or more might cause her to remove all of her clothing and try to have sex with a rat-bastard.

*I*f you must do something nice for someone, at least insult them while doing it.

*B*ig things can start with a little gazebo and a little jailbait.

*I*t's best to avoid having conversations with strange, imaginary Gypsy men who randomly appear in mirrors and urge you to kill the people around you.

*B*eware of deadly explosions. They can *really* mess up your hair.

*A* good way to cheer up someone who's bananas is to buy her a nice little sundress to wear home from the asylum.

*I*f your motorcycle repair shop burns to the ground, buy a boat and run a charter business. If a super-model blows your boat to smithereens, buy a bar and hope for the best.

*E*very once in a while, just go ahead and slap somebody in the face, really hard.

*I*f you really want to attract the babes, say something sappy every now and then, and keep the same goofy expression on your face at all times.

*B*e extraordinarily smug
whenever possible.

*A* good way to wake yourself up at
work is to have a big, steaming cup of coffee.
Another good way is to have
someone blow their brains out while they're
on the phone with you.

**W**ear tight clothing when barging into someone's wedding ceremony to proclaim your love for the groom. That way, it's more difficult for security to get a good grip on you when they try to throw you out.

*B*e sure to choose a family physician who has a lot of experience treating social diseases.

*S*tarting your own fashion design studio makes your hair grow rapidly.

*A*void sharing incriminating, intimate secrets with openly deceitful, manipulative bitches.

*B*eware of your estranged long-haired brother.

*B*e sure a regulation rubber mouth guard
is firmly in place before administering
electro-shock treatment.

*A*void killing the father of your
unborn child.

*I*f you must kill the father of your unborn child, don't tell the dead father's seemingly normal parents that their dead son is the unborn child's father, because the dead father's seemingly normal parents may very well turn out to be evil, custody-seeking grandparents.

*I*n the event that you do kill the father of your unborn child, and if you must tell the dead father's seemingly normal parents that their dead son is the unborn child's father, and the seemingly normal parents do turn out to be evil custody-seeking grandparents, then at least avoid having an unreliable alcoholic as your primary character witness at the custody trial.

**O**k . . . If you've found it necessary to kill the father of your unborn child, and to tell the dead father's seemingly normal parents (who turn out to be evil, custody-seeking grandparents) that their dead son is your unborn child's father, and the evil, custody-seeking grandparents *do* gain custody of your unborn child because your star

character witness at the trial was
an unreliable alcoholic, then you should
not, under any circumstances, attempt to
avoid giving up custody of your unborn
child by plotting an elaborate fraud with
an openly evil, psychopathic doctor—who
happens to have a gruesome head wound—
and (yes) a deep desire to also gain custody
of that same unborn child of yours.

*I*f you find yourself in the immediately preceding situation, just give the damned kid away and concentrate on your photography career. In all likelihood, he will somehow find his way back to you in a year or so.

*A*lways fasten your seat belt securely
before attempting to run someone over
with your car.

*T*ake advantage of every opportunity
to expose your midriff.

*A*lways wear proper eye protection when drinking alone. You never know.

*J*oining a radical cult is an excellent way to meet people and make new friends.

$S$tart the new year with a bang.

$I$f you really want to get back at someone, hang yourself. That'll show 'em!

$P$retend you're pregnant.

*B*e sure there's plenty of chlorine in the pool. God knows what's been going on in there.

*I*f you can't decide whether to love someone or kill them, flip a coin.

*L*ooking for a new receptionist is an
excellent opportunity to exploit the
opposite sex by hiring someone based on
looks alone. Be sure not to pass it up!

*A* good way to seduce a guy is to make believe you're blind, then wait until he's within earshot, get naked, pretend to slip in the shower, and cry out for help. When he comes to your aid, press your moist, naked body against his . . . . That should do it.

*Y*ou don't need family and friends when there's a bunch-o-hookers who love you.

*I*f you're in the middle of a monumental and devastating life crisis, hang in there.
It'll be over in about an hour.
Two hours, tops.

*I*f you come home from work one day to discover your wife has, somehow, acquired an infant which she intends to keep and raise as her own, don't ask any questions. After all, it's good for her to have a hobby.

*R*ecruiting your boss's abusive ex-husband as a new client is not the best way to impress your superiors.

*F*eeling a little insecure? Buy a gun!

*D*on't tell anyone you're engaged until after the big fashion show.

*I*f you want to find out if a person is faking blindness, make goofy faces at them and see if they laugh.

*B*e careful when drinking grappa. It's rumored by some to have certain aphrodisiacal powers.

*I*f someone tries to blackmail you with skeletons from your past, just go ahead and choke them.

*I*f you get demoted, it probably has nothing at all to do with your performance at work. Assume it's because your boss was blackmailed into demoting you.

*N*ever let your ex-husband tie you up.

*S*ometimes being responsible for blowing up an apartment building—resulting in the death and injury of innocent people—can make a woman just that much more lovable.

*D*on't discard old suicide notes. They can be worth a lot of money.

*P*osition yourself on the far side of the
swimming pool before detonating
your explosives.

*B*e suspicious of job offers in
Hong Kong.

*A* good way to cheer yourself up the week after your wife's funeral is to get engaged.

*M*en old enough to be your father can be sexy—especially if they have really big houses and boats.

One way to try and get your ex-wife to come back to you is to set up a cable company in her town, then hire her advertising agency to run your ad campaign.

*I*f your marriage isn't working, consider a divorce. If divorce isn't convenient, fake your own death.

*Y*ou can't have a decent party for the survivors of a deadly blast without inviting the person who detonated the explosion.

*D*on't walk too fast when feigning blindness.

*A*ccessorize your leopard-skin striptease
ensemble by wearing a pair of matching
cat ears on your head.

*I*f you're a little short on cash, ask your dad for a spare $100,000 or so to tide you over until the end of the month.

*R*andomly insult the people around you.

*I*f your boyfriend asks you to meet him outside his house and, when you get there, just stares at you from his window with his wife, you may want to rethink taking the relationship to the next level.

*P*lay it safe. Use an extra thousand pounds of TNT when destroying structures that have been standing for more than twenty years. You'd be surprised at how much abuse those older buildings can stand up to, and you wouldn't want to be left with the embarrassment of blowing up only *half* the building.

*W*atch your step when exiting luxurious yachts.

*D*on't pay too much attention to your dead brother's ex-wife. Especially if you're the one who killed him.

*I*f a car breaks down in front of your house and the woman driving it asks to use your phone, let her. Just be sure to rifle through her purse when she's not looking.

*A*mong other things, amnesia can make you forget you're an asshole.

*D*on't drink, and drive, and propose.

*I*f you get sauced and run over a kid with your car, it's time to reevaluate your life. Think about it. You can really screw up your car that way.

*T*ell anyone who will listen that your boss is very ill.

*Y*ou'll find out who really loves you when it's time to post your bail.

*I*t's considered to be in bad taste to say things like, "Well . . . back to work!" minutes after your business partner has buried his wife.

*I*t is imperative that you wait *at least* three months after someone tries to kill you before you retain that same person as your psychotherapist.

*I*t is equally important to wait a good two to three months to date someone who tried to kill you.

$J$ust because you're in the midst of ruining someone's career doesn't mean you can't car-pool to work with them.

$M$ake the best of any injury or illness by using your ailments to manipulate others.

*I*f you're romantically interested in someone, buy the building he lives in and move into a nearby apartment.

*S*ometimes being kidnapped can be a whole lotta fun.

*I*f your wife is mentally ill, have her shipped off to the county mental facility. It's less likely that she'll be cured there, and it's much cheaper than private mental treatment. This will get her out of the way, and you can use the money you'll save to help pay for engagement rings for your next two or three wives.

*A* good way to get back at your mother is to not use her models in your company's photo shoots.

*A*ustralians are evil.

*T*he only thing worse than a deranged redhead is two deranged redheads.

*I*t's tough for a guy to date other men when he's married to a Russian woman with a child.

*T*he next time you have amnesia and start to recover your memory, act like you still can't remember stuff that you really can— just to mess with people's heads.

*I*f you make love to a person who's addicted to sex, that makes you an enabler.

*A*lways be polite when blackmailing a loved one.

*I*f you're being sued for discrimination, avoid pointing at your accuser and screaming slurs against his sexual preferences two minutes into your deposition.

**S**tart all relationship-ending conversations with, "We've got to talk."

**D**ate aging "Hardy Boys."

You should know that if you survive a deadly explosion, you may have very faint, almost unnoticeable marks on your face the next day, but they'll be completely gone the day after that.

$T$oday's friend is tomorrow's lunch.

$I$f you're loopy, it might be because you stabbed some guy when you were a kid.

*I*f someone tells you that they love you, a good response might be, "Well now, that's your problem, isn't it?"

*N*ever base a relationship on lies and deceit. Just kidding! Dishonesty should be an integral part of any relationship.

*M*ake liberally slanted, vague references to current events whenever possible.

*I*f you're going to make out with your boss at the office, be sure to shut the blinds.

$I$f you don't have anything nice to say, say something nasty and rude.

$W$hen you leave someone to die of carbon monoxide poisoning, be sure to shut the door tightly on your way out.

*W*eigh down your kidnapping victims with heavy diamonds so that it's difficult for them to escape.

*E*avesdrop.

*D*on't date drug dealers . . . unless they're really good-looking . . . or have a lot of money . . . or unless you can gain something from it in some way . . . or . . . oh hell, go ahead and date drug dealers.

*I*t's hard to get back into the daily work routine when you've just recently come back from the dead, so take it slow.

*B*eware of doctors with *way* too much time on their hands.

*S*ometimes love can be wonderful.

*S*ometimes love can hurt.

*S*ometimes love can dress up in a wig and run you over with a car.

*D*on't get too close to people in comas. Sometimes they wake up and try to choke you.

*C*heck thoroughly behind your walls for creepy, peeping handymen before disrobing.

*A*void handing pointy objects to deranged, psychopathic, bomb-planting killers.

*I*f you must hand a pointy object to a deranged, psychopathic, bomb-planting killer, don't take your eyes off her.

*I*f you hand a pointy object to a deranged, psychopathic, bomb-planting killer, and you must take your eyes off her, after doing so, under no circumstances should you place your hand palm down on a flat surface, within striking distance of said deranged, psychopathic, bomb-planting killer.

**W** hen removing a pointy object from your hand, grasp it firmly and pull upward while rotating it clockwise.

You have to take the good with the bad. If you decide to marry a charming millionaire, his bitchy daughter comes with the territory.

*D*on't trust anybody.

*T*rust everybody.

*I*f you get fired, get drunk.

*B*ecoming intimate with a married, gay man may seem like a good idea at the time, but you may come to regret it.

*I*f your doctor sticks his tongue in your mouth, he may be carrying the ol' bedside manner a little too far.

*E*vidently, if you're a freelance photographer, you don't ever have to work.

$I$n order to get ahead in advertising, try to devote at least five (but no more than ten) minutes a day to actually doing your job. Use the rest of your time to ruin the people around you, and have sex.

*I*f you want to get your business partner's attention, remove all of your clothing.

*N*ever forget your roots. Not "roots" as in heritage. I'm talking about your *hair* roots. If you neglect them, they can really mess up a good dye job.

One of the most effective insults is a "boomerang insult." That's an off-handed, seemingly innocent comment that you initially perceive as a compliment, but moments later comes back and hits you as an insult.

*I*f a woman blackmails you into getting married, try to make the best of it. Make a deal with her: You agree to buy her furniture and stuff, and she agrees to annoy you as little as possible.

**A**void telling your fiancé that you don't love him. He may have a problem with that.

**S**leep with your ex-fiancé's new wife's dad.

*T*ry to keep life interesting and exciting. Every once in a while, approach a friend, or even a stranger, and get right up in their face and yell, "YOU FILTHY BASTARD!"

*I*f you aspire to be a critically acclaimed writer or novelist, don't give up. Strive toward your dream and hold onto your convictions for at least two weeks. After that, cave in like an old mining shaft and write advertising copy for a quick buck.

*A*n "Amanda" is not automatically a "Mandy."

*Y*ou can always be a little more understanding . . . but why bother?

*W*hen in doubt, bitch.

*B*e sure your company's health
insurance covers backstabbing.

*D*o things to try to keep morale high at the office. For example, encourage your employer to make Fridays "Casual Sex Day."

*M*arriage is a give-and-take kind of thing. Try not to overshadow your spouse by blatantly achieving more than your mate. For example, if you've recently ruined several people's lives, let your partner ruin the next few. In turn, if you have just blackmailed someone, allow your partner the opportunity to torment the next victim.

*I*f your husband of a few years blatantly cheats on you, sleeps with your sister, puts you through a horrible divorce, scams your inheritance money, weasels his way into your business, and makes your life generally miserable, to the point where you hate his filthy, rotten guts—by all means . . . keep his last name.

**W**hen your hair finally grows out and starts to look really good, chop it all off.

**W**hen fleeing the country on your 150-foot yacht, it's best not to tell your wife what's going on until you're well out to sea.

*P*arents will be parents. Sometimes they'll nag. Sometimes they'll be judgmental. Sometimes they'll commit you to a miserable insane asylum where you'll be bound in a straightjacket and heavily sedated.

*D*on't worry . . . . Be evil.

$I$f you're snooping through someone's confidential files and you encounter a locked file drawer, check underneath and behind the cabinet. Often, the key will be taped there.

*M*eet people for the first time soaking wet, wearing only a towel.

*E*xhale briskly and huskily whenever you're upset, happy, or sad.

*C*arry a comb when drinking because, for some reason, whenever you get drunk, your hair gets messed up.

*W*hen hiring a receptionist, look for someone with good typing skills, a polite phone manner, and experience as a hooker.

*I*f you're really serious about getting back together with your girlfriend, it's best to avoid having an attractive, scantily clad blonde move into your apartment.

*P*lead insanity to avoid lengthy and inconvenient jail sentences.

*A*void fistfights with the ex-husband of the woman you're accused of murdering— at least until after your trial.

*D*on't discriminate. Hire the bitchy.

*Y*ou don't have to be in love
to be engaged.

*I*f you blow up an apartment building,
don't be surprised if some of the building's
residents have trouble forgiving you.

*A*void giving relationship advice after slamming back six glasses of champagne.

*I*f you've got to fix your Harley, you might as well take your shirt off and do it by the pool.

*D*on't be afraid to design your own menswear line.

*I*f your dead brother's ex-wife has a working knowledge of computers . . . watch your back.

*I*f someone over fifty-five complains of being hot in a cool room, while looking really pale and taking short, labored breaths, you might want to at least ask him what's wrong.

*C*all your ex-wife "Baby."

*D*ate men with big, flashy yachts.

*B*efore leaving the laundry room, clean out the lint tray, turn off the light, and make sure your detonating lines are securely fastened to your explosives.

*I*t's important to try new things now and then. Every once in a while, just for the hell of it, be faithful to your lover.

*I*f you begin balding, comb your hair down straight over your forehead and pretend it's a hairstyle.

*I*f you're not careful, a person who stops by for a short visit may end up sticking around for a while and making your life miserable.

*I*f you want to have some real fun, get drunk and ruin your friend's engagement party.

*D*on't screw with Amanda.

And finally, a simple three-step guide to life:

**S**TEP 1: Love thy neighbor.

**S**TEP 2: Love thy other neighbor.

**S**TEP 3: Repeat steps 1 and 2.